LANDSICKNESS

THE SUNKEN GARDEN CHAPBOOK POETRY AWARD

LEIGH LUCAS *LANDSICKNESS*
SELECTED BY CHEN CHEN, 2023

Landsickness names and navigates a shattering grief in every possible way: through the pulse, via the intellect, from the shivering body and all its sweaters, over land, underwater, in the leaky vastness of night, in suffocating day, in a therapist's questions, with rage and somehow humor, too. I could not stop reading this collection. Its candor startles. Its speaker seems to hold nothing back about how ungraceful, how ugly the grieving has been and is. Though of course it takes tremendous craft (grace) to sustain, vary, and expand such an effect for an entire (beautiful) work. Such a gift, these spacious pages, this space in which any feeling, however unruly, can walk through and receive the honor of vibrating attention. I mean—this is love. Read it now.

—from Chen Chen's Judge's Citation

Leigh Lucas is a writer living in San Francisco. She has been awarded residencies at Kenyon, Tin House, and Community of Writers, and has been recognized with AWP's Kurt Brown Prize, as well as with a Best New Poet nomination, Best of Net nomination, and multiple Pushcart Prize nominations. Leigh's poems can be found in *Poem-a-Day*, *Frontier Poetry*, *North American Review*, and elsewhere.

LANDSICKNESS

BY LEIGH LUCAS

Tupelo Press

North Adams, Massachusetts

Tupelo Press
P.O. Box 1767
North Adams, Massachusetts 01247
(413) 664-9611 / Fax: (413) 664-9711
editor@tupelopress.org / www.tupelopress.org

Tupelo Press is an award-winning independent
literary press that publishes fine fiction, non-fiction,
and poetry in books that are a joy to hold as well as
read. Tupelo Press is a registered 501(c)(3) nonprofit
organization, and we rely on public support to carry
out our mission of publishing extraordinary work
that may be outside the realm of the large commercial
publishers. Financial donations are welcome and are
tax deductible.

CONTENTS

In my new life, I must learn everything again.

My friends are patient. They gather my coat and bag and say, *let's get something to eat.*

More and more, I manage on my own, lift my arms to wash my hair, thread my legs through underwear and pants, then let in wind, and speak a bit when spoken to.

Nights

Are each the same.

I roam the bounds of my tiny room, opening drawer after drawer,

Hoping to find something

That belonged to him.

I take the long, dumb walk to work,

Bring my bad attitude and forget my keys and wallet. My new uniform is a gray sweater that doubles as sleepwear. I smoke with my hair down so the smell stays.

Performing the required movements to remain employed, I lob needless lies at coworkers who dare come my way. I put a stapler in my purse.

At lunchtime my work-husband claims he no longer likes the salad place we've stood in line for every day for six months. *suck a dick*, I type in the company chat, and watch the cursor blink.

Back home, I crawl under the covers. My apartment is small enough that I can both shut the door and turn the knob on the stove without removing myself from bed.

This is helpful for my new lifestyle.

Shrines of his photographs, trinkets, and scraps of his handwriting form on my windowsills and dressers like birds' nests.

I lie in bed and stare into the messy monuments in search of signs from the beyond.

I dream I am
a woman under water, wordless and unmoving.

Sometimes, he is there. He holds his face and cries.

I am not a New Yorker and will not praise this scaffolding-covered city we keep building forever and ever, amen.

Only occasionally do I still see him, like when someone on a Citi Bike swerves playfully or shakes a mass of curly hair.

Walking the streets takes extreme effort, but even my bare-minimum life requires it.

When my phone dies, I am instantly and desperately lost.

Here's the rub. Fickle memory, swirling time, debilitating
seasickness.

Standing here at the red edge, arms full of unsent letters.
Looking up at the coconut tree, the long, serrated leaves,
coconuts near the top and dangerous.

We burn in one place   then maybe another.

I know I am embarrassing myself.

I try to calibrate the distances. Art requires careful theatrics.

Yes, be more cold.

Be ventriloquizer. Quoter.

Don't make a feast of cutlery.

Help. Is a beautiful thing to say.

Surrender.

When I had butterflies I couldn't shake he'd scoop me up and
lie on top and Squeeze Those Nerves Right Out.

So

what now?

I empty my pockets of odd little flyers and tear-off numbers for pest solutions and local handymen. I save them; some may prove critical at the end of the world.

The bravest friends still drop by. Today, their quest is laundry and to separate me from my sweater.

Alas, I am victorious.

I lie to my friends about laundered clothes, to my boss about work completed. I lie to myself that I wash my hands after I use the bathroom.

But sometimes I am honest.

The man I love

Jumped off a bridge on September 30th at 4 in the afternoon.

The man I love

      taught poetry

    to college students and kids at the Y.

He left a storage unit filled with duffel bags of paint, a city-wide scavenger hunt of bad graffiti, broken-hearted parents, a sister, and me.

He loved to sing and eat Kind bars and pet me when I'd sleep. Tall, still he liked to wear my clothes. His eyes made little crinkly noises when he smiled.

Light on his feet so when the music started, he'd be wiggling like electricity.

    He sank

    like a man

    of stone.

        The sun, I
            think,

                wa
                s in his
                  ey
                  es.

What happens to a body thrown?

Some believe numbers govern splashes:

A high Reynolds number makes them tall; a high Weber number makes them messy.

I appreciate attempts to lasso a slippery world, to number, measure, and taxonomize.

My own complex systems of ordering his belongings and memorizing minutia are for putting myself through punishing mental tests of recalling exact details of his poems, drawings and letters, of his feet, palms, and the curve of his back.

I transcribe his words into notebooks and save them to hard drives, inboxes, and every other place I know about on the internet. Tangible Items are arranged and rearranged in various safekeeping spots. Still nothing is ever safe.

When you possess a brain like cheese, things go missing quickly.

My mother grows accustomed to my panicked calls:
—*I promise, it's not lost. You'll find it when you're ready to find it again.*

I am pitiful at my sole pursuit:

                                              Nothing must disappear.

I love to think about his body. He was tall and beautiful.

Nice stems, I'd say. That made him laugh.

When nobody's watching I pretend it's mine. What a very nice body to have. Sight high, loping gait, shins to kick out, butt muscles contracting right up my back. Sinewy, tight. Large advantage lungs and a gullet with long bobbing Adam's apple. The most impressive of bodymachines.

I take it for a spin around the block, feed it strawberries, test out a big blasting fart.

It's my fantasy so I invite him to dinner. We sit at the ends of a table as long as the Last Supper's and gorge ourselves on chicken and plums. I pause to poke olives onto the tip of each finger. I drum them on the table and stroke my chiny chin chin. He accepts my challenge, threading asparagus through the webs of his fingers and crossing them over his head like Wolverine.

I hold his gaze and approach his end of the table slowly.

It's time to have a little chat, I say. Then I grip his one cold ear and howl into its endlessness.

Peppering him with questions, I say how is it, what's it like, how ridiculous do we seem to him.

He is careful to never give away the ending.

Good talk, I say, good talk.

I pin down his poems and threaten the shredder so they'll give up their secrets. But they are just more evidence of what I already know:

His poetry is unruly and electric.

Mine,

a child's hand in a fat grip on a fat crayon, puncturing crêpe paper. Be gentle, dear. You have to say it sternly.

A simpleton-philosopher, I seasick between: I knew this would happen (rock). And, how could it have (rock). Between: I knew him as well as I could know someone. And, I didn't know him at all. (Rock, rock.)

I try Emily Dickinson. The sticky letters fling like pearls when I round the stairs, they slip from my nose and cry help from the kitchen.

I try to replace a few like *carriage* and *scarcely*.

If I don't collect them quickly, I worry I'll wipe them up with a sponge. I was once so deft with a sponge.

My Adult Friend the Grief Therapist sends me mail. This one is called Bereavement After Suicide.

> Q: Can suicide be prevented?
> A: It depends.
>
> Q: Should suicide be prevented?
> A: It depends.

Scientists study depression in rats.

How we tell they have it and how bad they have it:

we drop them into a bucket of water and see how long they paddle.

He is twenty-seven-and-a-half. He is on the bridge. Twenty-seven-and-a-half, it's windy, and there will be no weather, just water soon.

He is twenty-seven-and-a-half and is wearing windy clothes and his face is windy. There is a sheen on this image. It carries on for minutes.

Now it zooms out for a wide angle. Everything goes still. A thing very small and faraway slips into the water. Swiiip. Not like a knife. Nothing like a knife.

The water doesn't move like blood because it moves like water.

A splash is a sudden disturbance

Caused by a solid object. Suddenly it hits

The surface.

The radial jet comes up first, around the border of the object. Wide

To soak the bystanders.

The object

     descends

Leaving air in its wake.

Impact speed, shape, and weight factor into the depth of the air cavity.

The cavity collapses inward under the pressure of the water around it. Water rushes to fill the cavity and in the rush, excess water shoots up and out. This is the jet.

The larger the cavity, the bigger the rush to fill it.

Humans, as far as objects go, are hydrophobic. This adds to the splash.

Kerplop!

The bloody part came and the audience went giddy, ripping their plush seats and dripping sweat on the floor.

Inventing every line on the spot, I wear Herculean tights. Dogs wait outside the theater doors.

The final note I hold's unending.

At the funeral, his other former girlfriend gives the eulogy. I sit in the pew.

Sitting in front of me, and behind me, and also to both sides, are more former girlfriends.

Something heartfelt shared by Ex on the Mic sets off a chorus of sniffles among the Exes in Rows. They tuck their hair behind their little ears.

There are so many different people to hate, so I keep things simple and hate everyone.

Grief does not look good on me.

I know why he picked me, a novelty.

I wore Mary Janes and high-neck dresses and labeled the shelves "Tuna and Nuts" and "Breakfast Items, Soup." My hair was always squeaky clean.

Now I am someone entirely new.

A black dog, a broken heart.

I revel in being more like him now.

I put on my sunglasses and turn off the lights.

Sitting on the toilet where light can't peek through, I pretend the plunger's a white cane. My chin held too high and to the side, I run through gruesome imitations of anger, contempt, disgust, sadness, surprise.

The world will be unsettled.

I will unsettle them.

NOTES

Heraclitus inspired the line, "Yes, be more cold," in poem "Here's the rub."

Marguerite Duras's *The Lover* inspired the poem "He is twenty-seven-and-a-half."

Maggie Nelson's *Bluets* inspired seasickness in poems "I pin down his poems and threaten the shredder."

Mike Orkutt's "The Physics of a Cannonball Splash" in *Popular Mechanics* was particularly helpful for poem "A splash is a sudden disturbance."

ACKNOWLEDGMENTS

These poems, sometimes in earlier versions, were awarded or appeared in the following publications:

AWP's 2020 Kurt Brown Award:

> "The man I love jumped off a bridge"
> "The man I love taught poetry"
> "I love to think about his body"
> "My Adult Friend The Grief Therapist"

Frontier Poetry:

> "Here's the rub. Fickle memory, swirling time"

North American Review (James Hearst Poetry Prize finalist):

> "He is twenty-seven-and-a-half"

Poem-a-Day:

> "At the funeral, his other former girlfriend"

The Tusculum Review:

> "In my new life, I must learn everything again"
> "I take the long, dumb walk to work"
> "Shrines of his photographs, trinkets"
> "I am not a New Yorker"
> "I empty my pockets of odd little flyers"
> "The man I love jumped off a bridge"
> "The man I love taught poetry"
> "What happens to a body thrown"
> "I love to think about his body"
> "I pin down his poems and threaten the shredder"